ruin
&
recovery

amanda stephens

ISBN:0692125396
ISBN-13:978-0692

this book is dedicated to

Nina Navarrette
my reason for starting it

and

Kathryn Jones
my reason for finishing it

ruin
&
recovery

contents

so it begins   11

rocky   21

anesthetized   29

abscission   39

sr(k)w   77

so it begins

processing

abstract pieces
some rigid
some smooth
spill out before me on my bedroom floor
a purge of the years
heaving
desperately
to get them all out
to clear the space
and try to make sense of it all
fit the pieces together
even though most have no compatible borders
it's a test of patience
a test of will
to see if i really can endure
and evolve into the big picture

<u>daniel</u>

Your smile
could light the darkest depths,
was as encompassing and powerful as the sun.
Your smile could save me.
It could save anyone
except yourself.

I miss you.
I miss the time we had but didn't share.
I always said
in life I have no regrets.
You made me a liar.
The time we didn't share is a chasm of regret
deep within my heart.
I feel the space.
I can never fill the space.

I knew you your whole life.
I wish I couldn't say that just yet.
But wishes in wells are just pennies in water,
sometimes if you're lucky a dime.
I would give everything I have to give
if I could insert myself into the time
right before you made your last decision.
I would try to change your mind.

<u>the first suicide</u>

It doesn't get any easier.
The levels and layers of pain are infinite.
It has been nearly 2 years.
You think that it wouldn't hurt as bad.
It's always a different kind of hurt,
a new hurt.
I never before encountered the 2 year anniversary of
your absence,
Now I relive it twice as hard, and twice as long --
The moment we lost you.

Etched into my memory like a laser into steel,
I remember every moment-
The seconds seemed to brake,
Mixed together into a strange pot of emotion,
a strange pot of time.
Mixed up
and swirled together.
A stew of shock and sadness.
Trying to hold it together was much easier than one
would think,
because it was incomprehensible.
Hearing the news of your death while simultaneously
celebrating someone's life;
It made no sense.
It made no sense at all.

Life.
And lack thereof.
It's the ultimate lesson in acceptance and surrender.
For some reason I thought those lessons might come in a
nicer package than this,
and that's not asking much at all.

<u>my second suicide</u>

It spreads like wildfire,
an epidemic.
Sadness.
You decided to let go of your own
but you left it here for us.

Left us here
to pick up the spattered pieces.
The shattered and missing pieces
that can't be put together again,
at least not the way they were.

Then here we are
with your sadness and our own.
What do we do?
Follow your lead?
Put an end to this agonizing misery?
It just compounds
and trickles down
to the ones that we love.

You would probably like to think
that your sadness ended with you,
It didn't.
It grew.

<u>losing lorelei</u>

The worst part of loss is that
you lost someone,
the rest of the world didn't.
It keeps spinning
as you are reeling.
Insensitive.
Oblivious.
Forward motion
while your world has stopped.

It's inconsiderate,
It's rude,
It's of no consequence,
It hurts.

And then
you keep going
...if you're lucky.

god damn the sun

i am bending
but i'm not breaking
it might feel that way sometimes
being pushed and pulled
by the whim of circumstance
an emotional contortionist
taking center stage in the circus
that is my life

i feel more than ever
that there is a purpose
to all of this madness
a lesson to be learned
something to be achieved
i just have no idea what it is
i do hope that there is
something
otherwise life really is cruel
at least as cruel as it is beautiful
which scares me
because the beauty that I've been privy to
is insurmountable

in an attempt to comfort
she told me that her mum
once told her
"bad things pour down like thunderstorms
to test those intended for greatness"
i'm not sure I believe her
but her attempt to comfort was a successful one
i trust because she should know
it's tattooed on her back
"god damn the sun
god damn the light it shines
and this world it shows
god damn the sun"
god damn love

<u>never alone</u>

I feel a little crazy.
I'm not sure if it's the jet lag
or absolute shock of the past few weeks-
suicide
culture shock
purging
and parasites.
I need a space,
a quiet space
let it overcome me.

Life is happening.
It's swallowing me up in a rip tide,
drowning me,
reminding me that I am powerless.

A week to go
before I enjoy the comfort of my bed
and the safe space I've created.
I would love to enjoy it alone,
but I am never alone
even though it appears as I am.

stolen hour of stillness

It's 8 am.
Everyone's sleeping.
I woke up to pee and decided to stay up
because this is the very rare occasion
where the house is completely still.

It feels good outside.
You can hear nothing but
the crickets singing,
the birds chirping
and the air conditioner humming.
The still silence is a welcomed sound
after the utter chaos of India.

The grass is wet and the air is fresh and clean.
It rained during the night.
You can see the dew drops on the blades of grass.
I like it here,
in this stolen hour of stillness,
where all I can see is nature's colors.

There's such a peacefulness here.
Inside, too, for an hour or so,
then the kids wake up,
Danny wakes up,
my parents wake up,
and the monster that has overtaken xxxxx wakes up.
She's gone.
I looked into her eyes and I can't find her anywhere.
She usually shows up for brief moments,
but so far,
she's nowhere to be found.

For now, I'm not looking,
This moment is mine
It's all for me.
I found my way to the eye of the storm
I am calm,
I am centered,
I am free.

rocky

<u>mom</u>

Little girl Kathy
had her first sip of wine
and her first taste of love
bittersweet.
Just 15 years
of life to her back
and a bright, shiny future at her feet.
She and a friend
had a nice rendezvous
with a couple of boys from their school.
Drinking and laughing
and making out,
everyone's feeling so cool.
In a brief lapse of judgment and hormonal fit,
Kathy and Rocky wound up in the bed.
A quick toss in the sheets,
future still at their feet,
the wine had gone straight to their heads.
Everything's fine,
kids will be kids,
until one day a child bore her own.
Uh-oh, a baby,
she said to young Rocky,
then he left her there all alone.
Poor little girl Kathy,
A child of 15, pregnant in the late 70s.
No support from her family,
No support from her friend,
And no support from the young man Rocky.

the process in between

The father returns and I become the child.
Insecurities
are ruthless thieves.
Robbing me blind
of all the work I've done,
all the faith I've found,
all that I believe.
I'm cowering in the corner,
a shell beside me,
a molting mess.
I'm at the process in between.

One bully of a moment
powerful enough
to overshadow all the moments before.
Placid,
at peace in the home that I built,
until a stranger knocks on my door.
He's finally here to tell the truth,
to make amends for the past.
The strong woman that I've become,
without permission,
immediately becomes
the child who wasn't enough.

I close the door.
Please stay gone
until I'm comfortable in my new skin.

<u>the wait</u>

The weight is proving to be more difficult
than the wait.
With time
I've become used to this space.
Suddenly,
a shift as bold as thunder,
shakes me from my comfortable void.

He is filling this void
that's been here for so long,
with his name
with his face
with his words.
I sit like a child,
trepidatious and uneasy,
barricaded in solitude
until the next step comes.

The weight
is so heavy
for a girl to hold,
even heavier when she's a woman.

I wait for the test to arrive.

<u>negative space</u>

37 years have passed
but it feels like not a day too soon.
Everything has its space,
its time.

It's ironic.
Your absence was a blessing.
You were never there
but you shaped the woman I have become.
I guess there's value in the abstract,
the negative space.
It creates its own piece of art.

I'm picking up all of the tools
I've collected through the years.
It's time to use them.
Time to till my garden
and promote its growth.
Maybe I always knew this day was coming
even though I thought I had laid it to rest.

I'm praying for strength,
an open mind,
an open heart,
and am being the truest to myself
I have ever been.

This,
the ultimate opportunity
to fill the space
I thought
would never be filled.

dna

Today is the last day
that I am the girl who lives a mystery.
Tomorrow I will be the woman
who knows the truth.

It's as if some great fault has been stitched together,
some wound I've carried around with me for longer than
this life
has healed.
Everything has changed, though nothing really has.

Maybe everything doesn't boil down to psychology.
I don't know why I could even imagine that we've got it
all figured out
We know the right tricks,
we know the right medicine.
Maybe it goes far deeper than that.
Maybe there's more to it.
Maybe we do live lifetimes.

All I do know is that this is the first time in this
life
that I have felt so balanced, and happy, and in tune
with the universe around me
the sky,
the trees,
the people riding in the cars beside me,
I feel it
I feel all of it.

The one thought that I keep coming back to
amidst the whirlwind of thoughts and emotions
is
I'm glad I held on.
I wish that Daniel could have held on.
I wish he could have shared my vantage that
in the end,
life hurts,
but it also heals.

<u>the moments before meeting my father</u>

I thought yesterday was the most important day of my
life.
I'm paralyzed to my bed with the realization that
every day to come will be more important.

With each step emotion surmounts.
The weight on my chest grows
my grasp on control weakens
my breath becomes more shallow
until I become nothing.
I am simply here.
Aware of every single moment.
Every moment stamped in stone,
because every moment
is the most important moment
of my life.

It's peculiar territory.
This place that I've dreamed of,
wanted,
not wanted.
suffered for,
grown from.
This hole in me
about to be plugged,
after all of this time.
One little letter can change it all
From hole to whole.
From your telephone to my computer screen.
It all changes in an instant.
After 37 years,
one click between the 1,175,520,438
ticks and tocks
Time reveals.

anesthetized

<u>someplace special</u>

There's an epidemic happening
in my hometown.
A zombie apocalypse.
Junkies chasing
their obsession,
money for drugs.

Money.
I need money.
Drugs.
Give me drugs.

Soulless and sickly
infesting the streets of
Marion, Indiana.
You have arrived.
Welcome to
"Someplace Special"

<u>not even her son</u>

there is a very harsh reality that I may never speak to
her again.
already she seems like a faded memory.
the permanence of her disappearance is more of a
reality than the life she has been living.
she bolted straight out of a running car.
she's been missing for over a week.
homeless.
she left with nothing but the clothes on her back,
and by nothing, I mean nothing.
no clothes,
no money,
no direction,
no one,
nothing.

not even her son.

<u>this time</u>

This time,
it's raw
and it's messy.
It hurts.

This time
cuts to the quick.
It's a nail ripped off its bed.
A paper cut to the eye.
This time
is rough.

I am a strong woman.
Time has proven that
time
and time again.
But even though I have the strength
I don't understand how I'm supposed to hold
this weight,
the weight of seeing you sinking
while everyone's holding on to save you
and they're sinking with you.

Even when we let go,
we are far too submerged
to catch our breath.
We are dying
with you.

It's not an easy thing to witness,
a demonic possession of the soul,
a point of no return,
a time of letting go.

I never saw this coming,
I never wanted this for you.
My heart is completely broken
and I don't know what to do
to bring you back.
Please come back, I beg of you.

dis-ease

put the needle down,
let it all go
and just come home.

your babies miss you,
your momma's sad,
your poppa's a nervous wreck.
all the rest of us
just want you back,
you've been gone for far too long.

sick with worry
and dying inside
the eye of the storm of addiction.
it's ugly,
uglier than i ever imagined.

been in denial for so long.
not just you,
but all of us.

<u>down</u>

my heart is heavy
       my body is heavy
             gravity

             is

             strong

             today.

snake eyes

I am sad.
I am sad because she is a heroin addict.
I am sad because there is a man
who tells me he loves me
and he needs me
and he is oceans away
in the arms of his long time girlfriend.

I am sad because the world keeps begging of me,
keeps needing me,
but I am too tired to wake up before 4 pm.
I have nothing left.
I have nothing in me to give,
and no one to give me what I need.

The only bit of hope I have
at this moment
is that Hank is communicating to me
from beyond.
We've never met--until now.
"then somehow we've touched,
strange brother or
sister,
and we both understand that death is not
the
tragedy."
Snake eyes
meeting snake eyes
in the thick and heavy solitude of my room.
Finding each other in the darkness.

Pull me out of here.
I'm too tired to keep climbing.
I need to escape this place.

bad habits

I've been rebelling against myself.
Telling myself to fuck off -
I don't need to write
I don't need to wake up
I don't need to do anything
that I need.

Dousing myself in early morning spirits
until I feel the world spinning,
until I have no option but to sleep,
sleep it off.

I used to believe that being alone was healing,
now I find it frightening.
When I'm alone
I'm destructive.
Call it routine
from a few bad years
that's the only thing I can call it.

But today,
I feel okay.

I'm on the mend
I remember what happy really is.
They say it takes 27 days to break a habit.
What if the habit is years long
and roots deep?
What if the habit was born from
suicide
and addiction
more suicide
and overdose
schizophrenia
and bi-polar
and everything in between?

Thank god Jen is here.
Because like Samantha said,
sometimes it's good to have eyes on you.

abscission

<u>a certain death</u>

death is certain
but always a surprise
moments taken for granted
until the time
where
there are no more moments

<u>dead on the kitchen floor</u>

Rob is dead.
This sentence seems so ridiculous.

I got a text from Mom today.
I knew when I called her back I would get bad news.
I assumed it was Aunt Mary.
I wasn't prepared to hear that something had happened
to her,
so I kept going back to sleep.
I finally made myself face reality,
but it was nothing that I expected.

Sarah answered the phone.
She told me the news.
Rob's wife had gone to work at 7 am.
Adam, fresh out of rehab, went to his Dad's around 9
am.
Uncle John heard Adam screaming from Rob's house down
the block.
He went right over.
Rob was dead in the kitchen.
Rob was fucking dead on the kitchen floor.

A toxicology report is being performed.
The coroner found track marks on his arm.
He was shooting heroin.
I think it's now official that everyone in that god
damned town is on drugs.

Rob.
I hadn't seen him in years.
I ran into him at Wal-Mart the last time I was home.
It was good to see him.
Time --- it has its way with people.

robbed

you're gone
your whole life flashes before my eyes
becky in her prom dress
the perfect couple
i admired you
you probably didn't know
i never told you because i was embarrassed
you were just too cool, my older cousin
time passed
you grew
you became a father
adam
then jonny
and ryan

the boys
i watched them grow up
i'm 37
you're 43
i found out today that you're gone
i saw your whole life
the story of you
evolve, unfold
what a privilege
bittersweet

live in love

4 more hours to go
until i wake up for the funeral
until the house is alive
and ryder is on the bed
demanding—get up
get up!

i am awake
listening to dad snore in the room beside me
relishing the silence
of this very lively home
before the day begins and leads me where it may.

i sit here
listening to the sleepy, heavy breath of the people i
love most in life
contemplating death
and its ever-presence
never knowing
when it rears itself

life
is never knowing much at all
except
love

with all of the doubt and uncertainty of the years
i realize
the only thing i know at all in this life
is love

with that in mind, that's how i will continue
for the rest of my days,
the rest of the days of everyone i care for,
i will do what i know
i will love
love unabashedly
love without embarrassment
love without fear
love without anything but
my full hearted intensity
because in the end,
that's all we have.
that's all we remember.
that is all.

kyrah- my one true thing

Standing in a room
flooded with tears,
overwhelming sadness,
and grief.
Needham-Story Funeral Home,
Gas City, Indiana.
Tuesday, March 7
The United States of America,
Planet Earth.
My whole world,
Nowhere at all.

Out of nowhere,
like a flash of light,
a sunbeam bursting through the clouds,
there she came.
My rainbow.
Running with open arms,
Her little face beaming,
Her little voice, high-pitched filled with happiness,
"Aunt Mandeeeeeeeeeeeee!"

Kyrah.

In that moment,
the heaviest of moments,
nothing existed
but love
and pure joy
for the little girl that was running towards me.

It's been this way since the day she was born
and grows stronger with every single second of her
life,
and, as much as I have been wanting to believe it,
I now know
beyond a shadow of a doubt
that
it's true-
nothing is more powerful than love.
Nothing.

She is my lesson.
My love.

Kyrah.

She is
My one true thing.

aunt *****

"I'm living in the shelter." she said.
"I'm living in the women's shelter." she said again,
waiting for a reaction.
I didn't bite,
but she kept reeling.
"There's a rumor going around."
"There's a rumor going around that I'm in there because
I wouldn't fuck *****."
***** is her son.

The rumor wasn't true.
The truth is
she was manic.
In a fit of rage
she attacked her son.
He had to pin her to the ground,
and why there was a machete on the ground is beyond me,
but it happened to be within arm's reach.
She grabbed it and swung.
She nearly chopped off *****'s head.
She was sent to the looney bin,
only to be released to the shelter.
At least,
that's what I heard at my cousin's funeral.

the procession - take one

It's been a whirlwind few days.
Within a few hours of my arrival at home,
I was awake and at the funeral home.
Seeing Rob lying in the casket was completely unreal to me.
It still makes no sense.
I saw pictures of his entire life with our family and his friends.
I knew them all.

I saw Heather and met my niece, Caitlyn.
I saw Dylan.
He's so grown up. He has no idea who I am.
I talked to Toby again.
I saw Richard and Doodlebug.
Christy and Charity and their families.
Sonny and Carolyn.
I saw so many people who were not just a part of my childhood,
they were my childhood.
I even saw Rob.
I must have seen Rob 20 times.
He was walking and talking,
until I took a second glance and realized it wasn't him.
Maybe it was.

There is so much to remember.
So many details.
What I remember the most, though, is the amount of people
and the amount of love and family that was in that room.
It truly was unbelievable.
It's almost as if I hadn't realized how close our family was until a few days ago.
How important we all are to each other.

It rained.
Aunt Marilyn said that she was happy it rained
because she heard that if it rains on the day of a burial,
the person being buried automatically gets into Heaven.
If I believed in Heaven,

I would believe Rob is worthy of admittance through the gates.

The funeral was incredible.
It was a show of how important he was.
The place was full.
A second room had to be opened to fit everyone.
As his favorite songs played,
amidst the tears and sniffles,
the boys sang along.
Old soul tunes.
His boys.
He left behind his 3 sons.
There was so much care and consideration given to honor Rob in his final day above ground.
When I die, I hope that the sentiment put into my last day is half as special.
Aunt Marilyn did a good job.
Hell, they all did.

Toby was a pallbearer.
After 5 years of not speaking to Rob or the Home Corner clan,
there he was carrying Rob's casket.
I'm so glad.
It's terrible that years can be wasted with a grudge—
same for Rooney.
In the end, though, it was as though no separation ever existed.

The funeral procession was incredible.
There were close to 100 cars in the caravan.
Tons of dog trucks. I loved that.
We are a family of greyhound racers.
First Whelchel Bros.,
then Whelchel and Son,
until a few days ago when the Son died.

We drove from the funeral home in Gas City,
through the country roads to Home Corner.
Aunt Marilyn had the procession go through their neighborhood.
It's where he was born,
where he started his own family,
where he lived his entire life,
where he was King.
I lost it.

As we drove through the place that was most sacred to
him,
past the homes where he spent all of his time,
I was hysterical.
This procession was truly an honor.
I can barely think of it now without crying,
but I'll hold onto this giant lump in my throat
and dam back my tears
so the poor man sitting next to me on the
plane doesn't feel too uncomfortable.

We,
the 100 car caravan,
drove through Marion to the cemetery
where Rob was finally laid to rest next to his brother,
Randy,
and Grandpa Ray and Grandma Jean.

The hardest pill for me to swallow when someone dies
is that that the world just keeps going.
You lose a piece of yourself,
and no one even knows
or recognizes your pain.
Even worse,
they don't recognize the life that has just ceased to
exist.

It was different with Rob.
I had forgotten this about small town Indiana
        the manners,
        the respect.
As the procession made its way through two towns,
everyone stopped.
All of the cars on the street pulled over to the side,
the people on the street stopped, some kneeled.
The entire city stopped to recognize
the loss,
the sadness,
        the life.
That small gesture meant so much.
It helped the healing start.

Robbie Whelchel lived and he died.
Yes, this loss is devastating.
Whether or not you knew him was of no matter, though,
you stopped to acknowledge.
My heart swells with appreciation

and I am humbled by the kindness and consideration
of the people in the town where I grew up.

At Rob's gravesite
we all stayed until his casket was sealed
and he was lowered into the ground.
I've always wondered if our deceased loved ones
are handled with care in the space
between our goodbyes and their descent.
I've never had the opportunity to see.
It was settling to actually witness this,
to know that he made it to his final resting space
safely and carefully.
Though Rob and I didn't keep in close contact over the
years,
there is no denying the life we shared while I was
still at home in Indiana.

When Rob died, my childhood died in many ways.
I tend to forget that Dad's side of the family is so
important to me.
I had convinced myself that they weren't there as much
as Mom's side.
But, you know what, I have been so wrong.
I make it a point to visit Aunt Bea every time I come
home.
Uncle David, too.
But I never make a point to see Uncle John and Aunt
Marilyn.
I probably spent more time with them than anyone else.

It's weird, the things you choose to remember.

As I walk away from this terrible time,
I see my life back home a lot differently.
I guess you could say that I'm letting go of grudges,
too.
Yes, it's true that Indiana isn't the place that allows
me to thrive,
and yes, it's true
that I may not have too much in common with most of the
people there,
including my family,
BUT there are two things that have become quite
apparent:

1. My family is strong. We love each other in a way that I don't see with other families.

2. There are certain qualities of life that exist in a small town that are so important and meaningful. There is a humanity, a simple humanity and common decency that exists there that doesn't exist in the other places I've lived. It's almost as if the townspeople are a family. A big fucking dysfunctional family that might make no sense at all, but will stop for a moment on the side of the road without a second thought to allow your loss to be the most important thing in the world.

temporary paralysis

I'm in hiding.
The weight of worry
anchors me to the confines of my bed.
It's safe there.
Warm and cozy.
Anxiety melts into the mattress.
Horizontal is my peaceful position.
As soon as I attempt to rise
I'm paralyzed.
Anxiety mounts.
Pressure pushes me back down
to the place where nothing can reach me.

I have so much to do.
I leave for Sri Lanka in 8 days.
Nothing is done.
The laundry I need to do,
the trip I need to organize
all waits for me
like a monster
sitting, snarling on its haunches
ready to devour me.

It's just that life can be overwhelming at times,
For the bad,
for the good.

and then...

a child dies, a child is born

Dillinger was born.
Perfection.
Pure joy
Pure love
Pure peace
wrapped up in human skin.
I can't remember feeling so wonderful just from sitting
in a room.
Then,
the bottom falls out.
I receive the dreaded call from Mom.
I know to expect dread because she only calls when she
has bad news.
It's not her fault,
we just receive so much of it lately.

Steps away from the exit of the hospital,
the building that just housed the most joy I can
remember feeling in quite some time,
I was pushed into the cold world of loss.
Death.

Again.

This time it's William.
He's 21.
He's just a kid.
He's so full of life.
How can it be?
As my heart breaks and my brain scrambles,
I can't help but think of Aunt Mary,
One of the strongest women I know.
Nothing can make her crumble.
Not age,
not fear,
nothing.
Nothing except William.
He was her grandson.
He was her best friend.

I think this could be the thing,
the crack that makes her crumble.

Then I think about Granny.
I worry for her.

I start to worry for everyone I love.
I feel guilty for being so far away from my family.
I feel guilty for so many things
including still lying in bed at 2:30 pm,
and for having the great ability to sleep when I'm
distressed.
Then,
more guilt
for sleeping when I could be living.

2 days in bed
and the best thing I can do is sit
with the feeling of my skin crawling,
my hair standing on end.
The best thing I can do is sit and write
because sometimes,
writing is really all I have.

my last letter to william

If it's true that our one purpose in life is to love
and be loved,
then,
William,
you truly lived.

Ever curious,
spirited,
gifted,
creative,
full of love,
this is how I have always seen you
      and always will.
21 years of inspiration and joy.

Gone too soon,
no doubt,
but what an impact you made
for me.

My heart breaks and is full at the same time.
Time.
I wish we had more…

I love you,
mandy

<u>and, now, adam</u>

Adam's dead.

Just like that.

Rooney saw him at 7.
Just two hours later,
he was at a friend's house.
He said he wasn't feeling well.
He went to the kitchen to get a glass of water,
I'm not sure if he even had the chance to pour it,
he collapsed to the floor.
And just like that,
in one ordinary moment,
Ryan and Jon lost their brother.
And their father.
In less than a 2 year span.

We lost our cousins,
Dad and Mom lost their nephews,
the Whelchel's lost 2 of their clan
in less than a 2 year span.

Payton, just a few days shy of 2 years of life,
will never remember her grandpa.
That is not the biggest tragedy.
The biggest tragedy is that she will never know her
father,
yet she will see him in the mirror
every day of her life.
A ghost of her maker.
The ghost of tragedy
always with her.
She is the spitting image of her father.

Adam is gone
Robbed of his 30s
Rob,
his father,
robbed of his 40s.
Death is the biggest thief.

<u>the rug</u>

I was happy for a moment.
for many moments, actually.
For 3 wonderful weeks
I had no loss,
no sadness,
the rug stayed firmly planted beneath my feet.
I was happy.

I guess it was my reprieve.
A reprieve book ended by losing two young cousins;
First Will.
Later Adam.

I am hoping happiness changed me.

I have been so used to living life in sadness
that I forgot how it felt,
what it was like
to live life outside of it.
To truly be happy
and free.

Until Vanita turned 40

And we celebrated her
in Sri Lanka.
In India.
Man, we really celebrated.
We celebrated life.
and Love,
and Inspiration,
and Joy,
and Freedom,
and Abundance.

It felt good.
It felt so good
that when I returned
I almost forgot how it felt to feel any other way.
Like darkness was a word I said,
not something I experienced.

Until last night.

It came back with the news of Adam's passing.
That rug was pulled right the fuck out from underneath
me.

Here I sit.
The day after,
and I am trying my best to tap into,
to hold onto,
that feeling I had 2 days ago.

I know I can't be as happy as I was then,
but I also know I can't be as sad as I was then.
It's detrimental.
It's my own death.

So in the midst of this sadness,
and confusion,
and heartache for my family,
I'm trying my best to hold tight to the cause of this
heartache.
The cause is
Love,
and Support,
and Happy Memories,
and Moments.
Without them, none of this would matter.
Sadness would not be a result.

Darkness is lurking.
Just waiting
in the cracks,
in the crevices,
to push its way through.

I've got to figure out a way to make the light so dense
that darkness doesn't stand a chance anymore.
Because sadness will come.
Heartache won't stop.
And for me, and my family, the tragedy doesn't seem to
end.
I've got to soldier on and love them all until the rug
slips away again,
so at least they'll know,
and I'll know,
that we were happy
and it was worth it.

my transcendent tragedy

It's 4 am
I'm drinking whiskey from a tiny paper cup.
There are too many dishes to be done
so this time, the environment loses
to disposability.
At least it's not plastic.

I'm not drinking out of sadness, though I should be.
I'm drinking because I woke up after 3 hours of sleep
and I have to be up in 4 short hours for the funeral.

I woke up because
I dreamed I couldn't breathe.
It turns out I was, in fact,
having trouble
breathing.
Logic would tell me it's because I've been recovering
from a cold
and I just spent 24 hours in the germ infested, stale
air of
airports and airplanes
and because everyone in this house smokes
all at the same time,
windows shut,
in the dead of winter.

I, though, believe I couldn't breathe as a
manifestation
of all of my thoughts being trapped inside the tornado
of my mind
with no escape.
Bottled up like claustrophobic beans in a jar.
How many do you think are in there?
If you guess correctly you'll get a prize.
You can never guess correctly.

So,
I woke up with this urgency to write
and for the last hour,
that's what I've been doing,
writing, with no end in sight.
You see, there are so many beans in the jar this time.
So many beans.
Yes, Adam is dead,
and it's all very sad right now.

60

But, as sad as the moments may be,
there is so much happiness to be found.

I've been sad for a very long time now.
There has not been a shortage of sadness in my life,
no shortage of tragedy.
The recent past has been filled with
suicide
crippling accidents
drug addiction
suicide
overdose
schizophrenia
overdose.
Yes, some things listed twice,
because some things happen twice as much.

My heart has been trampled and beaten
and buried so deep into darkness
that I didn't realize
it was now where I lived.
My home,
Darkness.

But recently, something changed.
I took a trip,
Vanita's trip.
My therapist asked me
before I left
what I'd like to leave behind.
So I made a list
of all the things
and she took it.
She said I could leave it wih her and she
would hold it for me.
I didn't have to worry,
it had a new place to live now.
And, it did.

I left and I didn't feel a thing
that I remember feeling for so long.
In its place lived something new, but familiar.
It had a different face
much like someone you love but haven't seen in awhile
you know it's them, easily recognized, but different.

Happiness.

Something I used to know,
easily recognized.
It felt like home,
just had a different aesthetic.

Feeling happiness felt so good.
Like I could see the soul of everything,
the breath in everything.
Even inanimate objects held life
and hope
and possibility.

I felt it every moment of the trip for nearly a month.
A full month!
Unbelievable.
there was no turning back,
and,
then,
I was tested.
The second bookend to the library of tragedy,
First comes William,
then comes Adam.
But this time, something changed.
This-
Adam had become
my transcendent tragedy.
His life,
rather, his death,
it turns out,
would not be in vain.

I can't go back there-
to that space of all encompassing darkness,
to that space of uncontrollable tears
and misery of memories,
and wondering
Why me?
Why them?

I can't go back to that place of drinking to mask the
pain
Of tuning out,
Of giving in to the pressure,
Of sleeping too long
And being afraid of the littlest things
      afraid of people
      afraid of myself

        afraid of anything at all
        outside of the sadness.

I will not go back there.
I refuse.

Vanita said there are cracks everywhere.
There are cracks where the darkness tries to kill the
light.
You can't let it.
I can't let it.
I have to be a warrior.
I have to fight for the light.
She's right.
So, here I am,
because of her,
gloves on,
dukes up.

This time I'm filling the cracks with something.
I'm filling them with all of the beauty that gets
overshadowed by the storm of sadness.
The truth is that I have so much to be thankful for,
no matter what fucked up shit storm life throws at me.
The greater the tragedy,
The greater my capacity for joy,
and recognition.
So now,
In honor of Adam,
I recognize:

My sister.
She's sober.
She's lucid.
She smiles.
She let me hug her.
And she actually hugged me back.
I see her soul shine thorough her eyes.
I see her be a good parent.
I hear her daughter say,
"Mommy's brain is fixed."
She sits here beside me and breathes.
She is alive.

I talk to Toby.
I have my brother.
I've missed him.

It's good to have him here, in my life,
actively living like we used to.

I have my family.

Ryder says I love you
and wants me to hold him.

Kyrah is happy.

The sky is vast and the stars shine.

I have so much.
I am so blessed.

So, yes, this time is a time of sadness,
but it is also a time of much more.
It's a time of no turning back,
it's a time of recognition,
it's a time of love,
of family,
of honesty,
of support.
It's a time to transcend the death grip that has been
squeezing me lifeless.
It could be the most important time of my life.

In case of emergency,
Place the oxygen mask over your face before helping
others.
The bag may not inflate, but the flow of oxygen is
there.

Thank you, Adam,
for the gift of understanding.
May this gift you've given flow through my veins for
the rest of my days,
and may your legacy be associated with that
resurrection
and happiness forever.
All of my love, cousin.
You will be missed,
but even more than that, you will be remembered,
and loved
and honored
and cherished.
Perspective.

take two

Today I walked a familiar path,
deja vu.

Walking up to the casket,
Seeing the same faces
wearing the same veil of emotion
        shock and sadness.
There they stood,
        Uncle John
        Aunt Marilyn
        Jonny
        Rooney
but instead of Adam and Diana
stood Becky and her husband.
This time Adam was in the coffin instead of his dad.
It is now 2017
instead of 2015
Everything else was the same.

27 years old
He had a heart attack.
His heart stopped working.
The irony of it all is that he was trying,
he was attempting to become healthier.
Going to the gym with my Dad,
working on getting stronger.
And for his efforts,
        this.
As I sit here trying to catch my breath
I wonder if this is how Dad feels when he breathes.
He has COPD
It's a lung disease.
He says he doesn't need the breathing treatments
even though he's been prescribed oxygen every night
and he continues to smoke.
We, in our family,
have a way of pretending things are better than they
are
when things are at their worst.
It's hard to believe a thing we say.

That's why it's so shocking to hear Aunt Marilyn
confess
that it's just too hard
and to hear Uncle John apologize

for not knowing what to say when I called to say I love
you.
Maybe this,
for us all,
is our transcendent tragedy.
The one where we stop all of the bullshit,
where my tight lipped loved ones finally start
expressing themselves,
finally start telling the truth.
Where I finally learn that I can feel sadness but not
live in darkness.
I'm so fucking sick of being sad.

<u>hard limes</u>

You can always count on ***** to be inappropriate.
Standing at the back of the funeral home,
Kyrah at my side,
he runs into me.
I give him a reluctant hug.
The reluctance doesn't come from him personally,
but from the words that escape his mouth
every
single
time.
Loud and nonsensical.
Embarrassing and infuriating.

He shows me his tattoo
He got it yesterday.
I can't remember the picture, but I do remember the
quality
It was surprisingly good for a Marion tattoo.
It read "Hard limes"
The artist forgot to cross the T.

The tattoo covered his scars, he said.
I guess that's where he shot heroin.
He overdosed a few days ago.

He said after he got news of Adam's death
he vowed to never do drugs again.
He got out of the hospital and found 2 fresh rigs in
his coat pocket along with some money,
he threw the rigs away and used the money to get the
tattoo.
Hard Times- with the cross missing from the T.

He said that doesn't stop him from getting bat-shit
drunk.
As a matter of fact, the night he was released from the
hospital
he got so drunk that he didn't know what to do.
He said he had to deal with Adam's death somehow.
I believe him.
I also believe what drives his addiction goes far
beyond Adam's death.
He said he got so drunk that he wanted to fight,
so he started fights.

He also said there was a girl standing at the bar, bent over,
no further away from him than I was now.
Kyrah, too.

Kyrah.
My sweet angel of a 9 year old niece
was standing in front of me cradled by,
what was just a few moments ago, a loving embrace,
but had now turned into protective fortress from the insanity of *****.
I don't use that word in jest
He could truly be insane.
Mental illness runs on Dad's side of the family.
Unfortunate genes.
I digress…

So there this girl was standing,
bent over the bar,
"No further than I am standing from you now,
so I whipped it out
and I stuck it in
and I smacked that ass.
By God, I smacked that ass hard, Mandy…"
I shield Kyrah's ears and shudder in disbelief
though I know better than to underestimate him.

He continues,
"I smacked that ass so hard
and I didn't even care that her man was standing beside her.
I didn't care"

I believed him.
What I couldn't believe is that his eyes were clearer
than I can ever remember seeing them,
at least since we were children
playing at the trailer park
unsupervised with the shot gun
and those damn, stinking ferrets.
His speech just as clear.
He said he gave up drugs after his overdose,
After being a heroin addict for years.
He started using at the same time
as my sister
and my cousin, Rob
and Rob's son, Adam

whose funeral we were standing at now.
Thankfully, Adam didn't die of an overdose like his
father did a year ago.
It was a heart attack.
And most thankfully, my sister has been sober for 6
months after years of a demonic possession.
Drugs are the Devil.

I know it's possible,
sobriety,
But at this moment, I can't acknowledge it or encourage
him
because I'm too busy trying to shield Kyrah's ears from
the maniacal words marching out of his open mouth
and oozing all over the funeral home floor.

I'm too busy trying to make sure it doesn't rub off on
her,
the insanity
There's been too much of that in her life.
She's only 9.

<u>mamaw's hands</u>

I look down at my hands
and I remember Mamaw.
Ashland, Kentucky,
standing in her kitchen
Granny singing with her sisters,
Mary
Inas
Bobbi.
Singing in harmony,
the women cooked,
breakfast
lunch
dinner.

Papaw playing the guitar on the front porch
after coming up the hill
from a long day's work with Uncle Bob.
Cousin Julie on the banjo.
Music danced in the warm Ashland air
with the fading aroma of Kentucky home cooking.

I remember Mamaw's hands.
Disproportionate marbles in the middle of her fingers.
Gnarled,
curled and crooked from decades of use.
Wrinkled skin,
tough and firm,
covering her fingers that could never quite straighten.

They looked so different from mine.
My young little hands.
Delicate
Not even ten years old.

Mamaw lived to 92.
Papaw followed soon
presumably from a broken heart.
Then
Aunt Bobbi,
Then
Aunt Inas.

Granny's still singing.
Aunt Mary's still singing,
and I'm still here,

so far.
I have lived 38 years,
and the one thing I notice
above all,
is my hands.
Knuckles large,
fingers curling
my skin a reflection of the years
covering the fingers that can barely fully straighten.

Years of use
beginning to show.
Each line,
each dent,
a moment of my existence encapsulated.
I have the epiphany that someday
I will die, too.
All I can think is that
I am not ready.
And,
I wish I had appreciated how beautiful my hands once
were.

last lunch with aunt mary

Funny how a particular type of paper towel can remind
me of her,
Aunt Mary.
The kind that's soft and durable enough to be a cloth.
It's been around my entire life,
this particular paper towel,
just like her.
She's in my first memories,
my happiest memories.
Granny's sister,
one of my first caregivers,
one of my first loves.
She is one of the most influential women in my life,
One of the strongest women I know.

Singing Froggy Went A-Courtin' for hours
all of the way from Indiana to Kentucky.
Singing that song over and over
        Froggy went a courtin',
        He did ride,
        Mmmmm Hmmmm.
        Mmmmm Hmmmmm.

        Froggy went a courtin',
        He did ride,
        sword and pistol by his side,
        Mmmmm Hmmmmm
        Mmmmmm Hmmmmm.

There are so many little memories,
little but lasting-
The jar of pens next to one of the two rocking chairs
where she and Uncle Clyde would sit.
That could be where my pen fascination started,
where my love for writing started.
For as long as I can remember
I've been on the search for the perfect pen.
I still haven't found it, though some of them come
close.

The framed print of two little boys standing next to
each other
in overalls-
"You been farming long?" asks one to the other.

They were just old enough to stand steadily on their
own two legs.

The ceramic artwork that hung on her wall,
there were four pieces,
circular plates,
each with a landscape representing one of the four
seasons.

The swing set that sat at the top of the hill.
We used to roll down that hill in the summer,
sled down that hill in the winter.
It seemed to be a mountain back then.
The swing set still sits there nearly 4 decades later.

All of these memories,
      so many memories,
and she doesn't remember me at all.
The last time I went home
for Adam's funeral,
we stopped to visit her
as we always do.
This visit was different for a few reasons.
Number one being that she no longer lives at home.
96 years old and finally moved out of that little white
house on the hill
to the nursing home where Granny now lives, too.

Number two being that she had no clue who I was.
She looked at Mom and said -
      "I don't think I've met this one before.
      She sure is sweet."
A stroke has ruined a piece of her.
I also blame William's death.

As I turned away
trying my best to fight the tears,
they just kept streaming
because I knew that this would be the last time I would
see her.
I cried because one of the most impactful people of my
life
didn't remember the impact she had.
I cried because I've never had this experience
of mourning the death of someone
sitting right in front of me.

<u>take 3</u>

And then there were three.

Here we are again.
I know this place well
Needham-Storey Funeral Home,
Gas City, Indiana.

With time, people are bound to die,
yes,
but the bulk of my visits have occurred over the past
two years.
It started with Rob.
Then, a year and a half later, Rob's son,
Adam.
Now 6 months later,
Uncle John.
Dad's brother and best friend.
Rob's dad.
Adam's grandpa.

He died of a heart attack.
Just 2 weeks prior, Mom had her own.
She died, too,
but they brought her back.
Defibrillated on the way to Fort Wayne Lutheran
Hospital.
Resurrection in the helicopter
I haven't been able to write about that,
I don't think I will.

Uncle John wasn't as lucky.
I didn't see it coming.
None of us did.
I saw him when I was home for Mom's recovery.
I waved.
It was cold and I was busy so
I told Aunt Marilyn to tell him I'd see him next time.
And I did.
But I didn't think it would be like this,
in this room,
at the Needham-Storey funeral home.

I didn't cry today.
The tears would arrive tomorrow at the funeral.
Today I was just numb

and noticing the similarities of my previous visits
here.
Sitting down,
facing the family
except this time there were three—
      Jonny, Rooney and Aunt Marilyn
standing tirelessly next to Uncle John's lifeless body
giving endless hugs
explaining the devastation
      over
      and
      over again.
4 hours.
I don't know how they do it.
I'm guessing they don't either.

I was dreading this trip.
Dreading seeing my dad break down again.
There is nothing worse than hearing your dad cry.
I've heard him absolutely hysterical twice in one month
that's two more times than I've heard him hysterical in
my entire life.
I made it, though.
If they could do it,
I could, too.
I made it out on the other side,
though I truly thought this was the one—
the one unfortunate incident that would make me snap
I didn't.
I didn't because love filled in the cracks.
It gave me a stronger foundation than I had before I
got there.

There's something beautiful about suffering.
I guess you could say I've learned
that my capacity for joy is only as strong as my
threshold for suffering.
The more I lose,
the more I become aware of the moments,
the seemingly mundane times,
the little happenings that add up and accumulate
into something…

A blizzard starts with one snowflake.

sr(k)w

<u>ripple effect</u>

I write it in the sand
so it sinks into the sea
and ripples all around this world
for all eternity

I love you.

<u>our love</u>

It was a love that fought
to stay alive,
a love that waited.
a love bound by blood,
a love that never hesitated.

It was nothing short of magic.
Fiery and intense,
Strong and surreal,
but more real than any other
I've ever experienced.

Our love.

future history

I remember the first time I saw your face,
face to face.
You walked into the room
completely out of place
with your style and swaggering grace.
You wore a red hat and a frown.
You sat, head down,
staring.
I stood, head forward,
sneaking glances of you for the first time
in my real life.

You left.
You left your lighter behind,
The Rolling Stones.
I kept it
for safe keeping.
A conversation starter for our next meeting.

We did,
we met again.
You didn't need the lighter,
you quit.
So did I.
We decided to pick up a new habit,
My favorite one yet
and the hardest to break,
We created the habit of
You and I.

<u>the poet and the muse</u>

One is here
One is there
Joined together
in the spirit of love,
breathing
one eternal breath
in the corners of her mind.
Pangs of longing
encircle and enflame.
The relationship of the two,
tragic and hopeful
beautiful and grotesque,
the enchanted
and
the enchanter,
the Poet
and
the Muse.

<u>dream lover</u>

Hidden opposition
is the theme of our love,
a story with no happy ending.
Forces invisible,
some clearly seen,
draw the curtain between You and I.
Still,
we exist,
finding a way to communicate
in other dimensions.
My dreams,
always welcomed,
though most times not sweet,
are our time and space to be
the Us
that refuses to divide.

<u>steady as change</u>

I write letters to you
that you will never see.
Vacillating
between letting go
and holding on.

Emotions are volatile.
Emotions are fleeting.
But my love for you,
My Love,
is as steady as change.

the end

you always were my number one muse
i think of you
and the words just fall
right out of my mind
to the paper
so easily
they have since the moment we met

you gave me so much
you gave me everything
i never took the time to really reflect on it
i guess it hurt too much
to think about us
because us is something that I never wanted to end
what i didn't realize is that it hadn't ended
not yet
not until 3 days ago
they found you dead
in your bed
on the bus
alone
i suddenly understand
the true definition of the end
i wish i would have known
that there was still time
but the time was limited
i'm sorry i let you push me away

were you thinking of me, my sweet,
before you took your final breath?
was i one of the last thoughts to cross your mind?
i ask because i felt you
in the air
in my space.
sitting on the floor
unwrapping the memories
of us
that i swore i had put away for good,
left for dead in a box
in the furthest, darkest corner of my closet.
for some reason i pulled them out that day.

i felt it cover me
the feeling of you.
i hung your picture.
i wore your necklace.
i even wore your jacket to the show
that i didn't get to see
because of the call from lazie
telling me the news.

i thought for so long
that maybe it had broken,
the connection from your heart to mine.
i didn't feel you anymore,
like you had gone away,
but i don't think you went very far
because i swear i felt you that day
whisper my name
and visit my dreams.
i feel you now,
even though you're gone.
i feel you all over me

<u>waiting (for something that will never come)</u>

i'm not asleep,
but I'm still trying to wake up
from this bad dream.
waiting for someone to tell me
you're not dead.
waiting for you to go back to her,
waiting to still avoid streets
that i secretly want to travel,
waiting to hope that i see you
in the neighborhood,
waiting to anticipate what i'll
have to say,
waiting to show you
the woman i've become
since you went away.
i'm waiting, my darling,
for whatever it takes
to bring you back to life.
please come back to life.

<u>not invited to the funeral</u>

5 days gone
and still no news.
I don't think I'm invited to the funeral.
Jamie's widowed
Mary's pissed
and I'm sitting here in the shadows.

A decade I've known you,
It passed so fast.
Time is always quickest when you're looking
behind you.

<u>the funeral</u>

I wasn't invited to the funeral.
I still haven't decided if that was the best thing
for me.
We never had our closure.
I wanted to see you
one final time,
but maybe you didn't want me to see you
lifeless.
I might have been one of the few people on the planet
to see you truly happy,
to not have witnessed total moments of self-
destruction.
At least until the end,
That's when it began.
I still believe that is why you pushed me away,
never saying goodbye-
because maybe it wasn't goodbye,
maybe you held hope,
at least for awhile.

You married her.
You became a shell of a man
Lifeless long before you died.
I know you tried
but the synapses misfired,
and the medication was only making you sick.
You took a turn that I couldn't take
Lord knows I tried.

It is only me who believes
I didn't try hard enough.

<u>the reckoning</u>

been moving,
continually moving.
trying to outrun the thought of you.
it doesn't work.
i just find myself exhausted and more vulnerable
for the inevitable moment that you make an appearance,
sneak your way back in
to the very heart of me.
it doesn't matter what i'm doing,
or where i may be,
you show up when you want to.

i always see you.
but it's those moments that you see me
that leave me
sad.
heart broken.
full of regret.
kicking myself for the things i didn't do,
for believing that letting go is what you're supposed
to do.
that it's for the best.

all for appearance sake.
i didn't want to play the fool,
to keep trying,
to never give up
just because you did.
all of those things that you did for me
for all of those years.

i can't help but wonder
if i would have fought,
would you have lived?
would things have turned out differently?

<u>he is the air</u>

He is the air
He is everywhere
Thoughts at every intersection
Memories in every hall
I can't escape him
And I don't want to

I hear him in the radio
He communicates through songs
Of course he does
He knows that's how I'll hear him
How I'll know it's him
Sometimes he answers me
When I plead in the night-
Help me
Please
Help me
Help this hurt
Help me know you're here
I swear I feel you walking with me
Hovering above me while I sleep
Help me with this agony
Help me
Sweetheart
Please

He is the air
He is everywhere
I feel him though he's gone
My lover
The ghost
I can't escape him
And I don't want to

6 weeks gone

I search for you
every day.
Sometimes I'm lucky
and find new clues,
but mostly nothing,
dead space.
Dead.
It has become my least favorite word.
It carries too much meaning.
It carries nothing at all.

It's been 6 weeks
since I got the news.
Time.
The most confusing word.
It moves so quickly,
yet remains still.
It's as if no time has passed at all,
I still wake up
every day
with a weight in my chest
and a tear in my eye.
With a sea of unnerving energy
surrounding me.

I've been awake for both
the sunrise and sunset
for days on end,
and nothing changes in between
except the lines on my face.
Growing deeper,
etched by rivers of tears
forging their pathways
around my eyes.
My delicate skin stings.
An outward manifestation
of the constant pain I carry,
and always will,
because death has no end.
Until I meet my own.

4950

I drove past your house today.
It's as if the car was driving itself.
I wanted to stop
and look
and remember,
but it just drove away.

Memories came flooding back.
The dam was broken
by the familiarity
that I had avoided for years.
As soon as I turned onto Ethel
anxiety flared,
breath more shallow
with every rotation of the wheel.
Counting the houses with anticipation
until there it was,
4950.

You were so proud of that house,
it was just in the wrong neighborhood.
You did everything all by yourself,
it was yours.
For the first time in your life,
something was all yours.
It was beautiful.
Every wall,
every window.
it became my home, too.
We covered every inch of that house,
me and you.

I broke in.
I walked into your kitchen,
sat on your couch,
used your shampoo,
rested my weary bones on your bed.
All within seconds.
All without leaving my car.
My car just kept driving away.
Away.

I turned the music up as loud as I could bear.
A sound bath for the soul.
        I appear missing now.

        Shock me awake,
        Tear me apart...
another album by Queens to be my therapy.
They were always the perfect fit
when I was broken up over you.
I must have heard every song thousands of times.
And, what an ending to the tale,
it was Joey who found you
lifeless,
alone,
in bed on the bus.

<u>heart shaped potato</u>

In therapy
I spent an hour
painting a picture.
Watercolor.
Fluid like tears.
It was my landscape with you.
Cherry blossoms against a cloudless, blue sky.

Time was up.
I left.

Made a left on Magnolia
at the exact moment
Lucinda began to sing
Magnolia.
My sadness and doubt shifted
to happiness and certainty.
Synchronicity.
A blatant marker on my journey
to let me know
I'm headed in the right direction.

I pulled up to the Shoebox
and parked my car.
I opened the door
and there you were,
mounted on the wall.
Your face was the first thing I saw.
I knew at that moment
I was definitely where I needed to be.
The first edition of Inked Magazine.
My first edition of You.
When we fell in love,
When you were alive --figuratively and literally,
and we were happy
with our Stoli dirty martinis
and fresh cut flowers,
And all the conversations we shared
that spanned for hours,
And the love that lasts lifetimes
and beyond.

You wrote a note
on your stationery
I put the words on my ribs-

I love you.
I know you do.
I love you, too.
Always did.
Always will.

<u>he won't let me be</u>

He's here.
He's back
from the deepest caverns
of my heart,
from the darkest corners
of my mind.
What an astounding trick he plays
being everywhere
and nowhere
all at once.

I can't lose him.
I've tried.
He always finds his way to me.
He lingers behind
pulling me back when I get too far ahead.

My love.
His ghost
is here.
He haunts me
in my waking life
and haunts me in my dreams.
Though he left me long ago,
He just won't let me be.

<u>the witching hour</u>

i'm not sure why
it hurts worse at this hour,
but it does.
shot by shot
i try to run from the memory of you,
but i find that i only come closer.
in the wee hours
you haunt me.

i talk to you.
you take up space
even though you're nowhere to be found.
dead as a doornail,
so they say,
but more alive than ever in my mind.

<u>too drunk to be afraid</u>

it's nights like tonight that i understand him
far more than i ever wanted.

for no reason in particular
i keep going
beyond the place of acceptable behavior.
i hear tales of moments i can't remember,
lost behind a veil,
blacked out of my mind.
frightening as it is,
i reach for another
because i'm beyond the point of caring,
and that's the place i've been trying to reach.
a place where it doesn't hurt.
no confusion
no worry
no nothing,
almost not even a thought of him,
until i reach for the bottle and see his face.
i empathize.
i'm still too drunk to be afraid.

half sleep

mourning the loss of hope,
lethargy overcomes,
covering me securely like my favorite blanket.
gently enveloping me like my lost lover.
snuffing out the light.
it's all safe here
in the dark stillness.
peace.
no responsibility.
no forced smiles.
no forced words.
only silence.
floating.
only me

<u>it</u>

I heard you.
Hold on to something still,
You don't want me to be alone down here.
You are happy,
and sending love.

Moving slow
but way out of control.
I need help.

Feeling so lonely
I try to let go
but,
It holds me,
this ache
this loss
this missing you.
It keeps me company at night
It speaks to me when I'm alone
It comes to me in my dreams.

If I don't have
It
I have nothing.

tancho

you left his scent behind.
from your hair
to my pillow,
to a decade ago
at the oakwoods,
then onto strohm.

my eyes closed,
cheek against the fabric
breathing in all of the memories.
breathing them in as deeply as i could,
hoping that if i breathe them deep enough, they'll
never leave,
they'll stay right here.

one single scent conjures the ghost of you.
the ghost of us.
i'll never wash this pillow case again
so i can sleep with you once more,
until it fades…
please don't fade.

true blood

a picture hangs in my closet
of you between my parents.
a band-aid visible on your
arm.
i look down at my own arm to see the scars.

skin sealed
where blood once escaped,
from my veins
to your lips.

i'm not sure why we did it.
maybe because we wanted to live forever
within each other.
maybe because we wanted to taste every inch of one
another,
inside and out.
maybe because we wanted to be one,
two separate people
sharing the same life force.

a positive
a negative.
we could have saved each other.

we could have saved each other.

stampede

Unlocked
like caged animals,
the memories of you stampede.
Tromping over my heart,
dragging out a smile from suffering,
and a near inaudible whisper-
I love you.
I love you.
I love you.

Pleading.
Desperate.
As if I say it enough times
you will hear me from beyond
this life.
Making up for all of the times I held it in,
those words.

Like I was holding my breath,
I gasp for air,
filling my lungs for the both of us.

The stampede.
It comes when it wants to come.
I am defenseless.

It is slow,
and it is painful,
this time after you.

<u>your first dead birthday</u>

here it is,
3 hours into october 27.
your birthday.
your first birthday since you've been dead.

it's still hard to say that word in regards to you,
dead.
it's nonsensical and stings every time
because you are very much alive to me,
still,
always.
you're everywhere
every day
nothing has changed
in my heart.

i looked at the clock just moments before midnight.
i hadn't actually thought of you all night,
until then,
something within me went off,
an alarm in my heart,
a whisper in my soul,
saying
honor him
remember him
be grateful for him.
i always do
nothing is new.

i imagine i'll write a lot today,
think a lot today,
feel a lot today.
i'll try to keep it positive.
i'll try not to cry
too much
because today is a happy day.

it's the day that you were born.
the day that changed my life for the better
forever.

do it for the kids

driving to work
your song came on my shuffle
one of my favorites
it reminds me of a very specific time
you with fire engine red hair
shirtless
tailored pants
sitting on a stool
so simple
so sexy

you gave me a picture from a photo session
around the time that we met
it was wet from the bubbles in your laundry room
it flooded
you desperately mopped
while i tended to walter
that may have been the night he peed on the bed

you left me for mary
do it for the kids
one last shot
i did it for mario
trying to convince myself that i wasn't dead inside
trying to convince him that i didn't care about you
i threw the picture away
all the while carrying around words
words that came spilling from my broken heart
words that were inspired by you
and your love
and your belief in me
and my unconditional love for you

if you love something set it free
but hold onto those pages
until you see him again
you know you will
and i did.

you came back
long after i threw the photograph in the trash
long before i heard the song on my shuffle
and smiled instead of cried

i actually allowed the song to play the whole way
through
it was the first time since you died
and i swear i felt you
some sort of electricity
making my hair stand on end
making my fists curl
almost as if to hold my own hand

i like to think that it was you
moving through me
even if only in a memory
of the big bang baby
that you created with me

<u>the lesson</u>

its 4:24 am
i sit here
alone
well, not completely
i'm accompanied by whiskey
and words not spoken
feeling lonesome
and defeated
tired and weary

i want to sleep for days
sleep until this nightmare goes away
that's what life has become
a nightmare
scattered with bits of happiness
and distraction
liquid escape in a well that runs a few ounces deep
i don't know what to do anymore
i've suffered through suicide
addiction
and sudden death
i didn't think it could get worse
but it has
life showing me that meg was right-
i still dream too small
i often think
would the early 20-something girl in me
who sat at the ritz nearly every night
have been able to see her life 10… …15 years from then?
outside of austin?
outside of childhood?
outside of the space where she thought she had reached
her lowest?
people talk about making goals
a 5-year plan
but seriously, that's bullshit
impossible
we have no say in what happens five minutes from now
let alone five years

try as you may
to walk down a certain path
life is a hurricane
a tornado
an earthquake

lifting you
shaking you to your core
moving you when you had no desire to move
at the time you least expected

it's 4:33 am
I have lived 39 years and 4 months
and through it all
through this tumultuous existence
through the thick of it
the good and bad of it
the only thing that matters
is to be happy
do whatever it takes
to truly be happy

fuck the rules
fuck the logic
fuck yourself sometimes
just find a way
to be happy

<u>since friday</u>

I've been pretty lucky,
one could say.
I haven't had a break down since Friday.
It's Wednesday now.
I came pretty close one morning
on my way to therapy,
the perfect time for a breakdown
actually,
but I wouldn't let it happen.

I think I've become allergic to tears.
Any time I cry my left eye throws a tantrum.
I guess because it's the one closest to my heart.
It gets back at me for the torture
while I sleep.
I wake up unable to see,
swollen lids,
red and raw.
Burning.
Delicate to the touch,
hideous to the sight.
I think I've simply cried too much.
My face is sick of it.

It's interesting
how I need to erase reminders of him,
yet honor his memory and keep it alive.
The wound is still fresh even though the injury
happened over 7 months ago.
7 months.
I still feel it like it just happened,
when I allow myself to feel.

I'm not sure where the phrase came from-
"Good grief",
because, grief,
it's never good.

<u>my sadness, the secret</u>

i keep my sadness a secret.
time has passed along with people's understanding.
they think i'm okay,
but I'm not.
i'm still heart broken.
i'm still tortured,
still confused,
still crying.
still searching for signs
or messages that will never come.
still holding onto hope that you are with me
and that you hear me,
still holding on to non-acceptance
because i refuse to believe that you are gone,
gone forever this time.
But you are.
And that reality hits me like a ton of bricks,
like a sucker punch to my heart,
several times a day,
still.

8 months you've been without a breath.
8 months i've been in denial,
refusing to believe
that this is how it ends.

the seattle scene

I thought I'd try to ignore today.
I never understood why people feel it necessary to
acknowledge
an anniversary of a death.
Still, they do.
They did before I had a chance to.

I woke up to messages,
sweet messages,
of sorrow for me,
for this day.
Eyes barely open,
I hadn't even had time to think about losing you yet.
As the moments moved forward,
it sat inside,
the memory of you,
actually the memory without you.

Pushing forward
forcefully,
an aneurysm ready to burst,
then,
BAM!
at breakfast
it burst all over my latte.
There I was,
crying in public.
My first time in Seattle
with the same person who was there when I got the news
that you were gone for good.

Gone for good,
I never understood that phrase in regards to something
that was never bad.
You weren't gone for *good*,
you were gone for the *worst* I'd ever experienced.
Day drinking began right after my public display.
Apropos for the occasion.
I would drown my sorrows,
I tried to drown them but they wouldn't die,
they just hurt less.
I numbed the pain.

Then washed it all away
in a bathtub with Samantha

while Stella slept on the couch.
I made it through
the first anniversary of the death of you.

zero gravity and lavender

I smell him everywhere.
The overwhelming scent of a memory
that I can't quite recall.

My bathroom was just painted,
the aroma of fresh paint and lavender hit me like a ton
of bricks.
It takes me somewhere,
back to you,
back to your place on Ethel,
Our place on Ethel.
Sherman Oaks, California
United States of America.
Home
for awhile.

It hits me hard
because it's so familiar,
yet I can't quite recall
what it is about the scent that takes me somewhere,
takes me back to you.
Is it the fragrance of fresh beginnings?
Is it the scent of 4950?
new home
new paint
new you
new us
same lavender.
Lavender was always a reminder
of my time with you.
You gave me the introduction,
I fell in love with the aroma
Then I fell in love with you.

I keep breathing breaths so deep,
and so hard,
nearly suffocating
to hold onto this feeling,
the feeling of you in the room.
Holding on because I know the trigger will fade
and leave me alone
without answers
without hope
without you.
In the space that I have learned to accept,

114

The space where loose ends don't get tied up
and love does not find a way,
where all the reckoning in the world
doesn't make it okay.

Where I fall apart
Where I lose control
and tears rush out like an undammed reservoir,
flooding me.
Overcoming me
with a sadness I try to accept,
a sadness that I try to turn into something different,
but it never goes away.
The only things that fade are the memories and the
truth
which only come alive when I least expect it-
in a fresh coat of paint.

Luckily it lingers for a few days.
For those few days
I remember what it's like to be loved
and to be happy in a home
and to believe in the concept of forever
and second chances
and happily ever after.

Most importantly,
I remember you.
Your voice
Your touch
The smell of cigarettes in your bedroom
and the way you felt when we slept together in your
king sized bed
beneath the crimson, velvet blanket.
And all of those pillows that I never remembered how to
properly replace
the morning after we threw them on the floor.
But I tried.
Day after day I tried.

I tried my best.
I hope you know.

thank you.

in loving memory of

Daniel Stephens

Brandon Fraley

Lorelei Wolf

Rob Whelchel

Scott Weiland

Adam Whelchel

William Story

Mary Opal Smith

John Whelchel

With everlasting gratitude to
my vast and unwavering support system

&

love and compassion to all of my family and friends who
suffered through these losses as well

Made in the USA
Monee, IL
05 September 2019